A Bridge Across the Pacific

Leaves for
Chen Zi'ang, Guan Yin, and Du Fu

By David Cope

Translations by Zhang Ziqing

Suining International Poetry Week

26 February - 9 March 2019

A Jabber Publication

Homage to Guan Yin, and to Chen Zi'ang and Du Fu,
Great Spirits at the heart of this meeting.

Deep thanks to the City of Suining and to *Poetry Periodical*
for making this journey possible.

Special thanks to Dr. Zhao Si, for your many kindnesses,
to Ray and the other young guides for your friendly and attentive
help— and to my fellow conferees, for your poetic gifts and camaraderie.

Front Cover photo of Chen Zi'ang statue at Chen Zi'ang Reading House in Shehong,
by David Cope, copyright 2019.
Back Cover photo of Du Fu in his Thatched Hut Memorial Garden in Chengdu,
by David Cope, copyright 2019.
Text photos: other than the photo of the author by "Ray," his guide
(known only by his "guide name," as he did not share his Chinese name), all
photos by David Cope, copyright 2019.

Thanks to Jim Cohn for his superb editing notes, and to my editor and publisher,
Jon Dambacher, for his incisive critique and suggestions.

The handwritten and printed manuscripts of this journal in key drafts are available
in notebooks, notes, travel materials, Chinese publications and flyers, all located in
archive, The David Cope Papers, at the University of Michigan Special Collections Library.

Acknowledgements: "From the Top Step of Guangde Temple" appeared in *Big Scream* 58 (2019)
and as a broadside by Multifarious Press, Chicago Ill.
Meditations, Dialogue, and Afterword essay appear in *Rabbit: A Journal of Non-fiction Poetry*
(Australia). The final version of "Waiting for dawn in a Beijing hotel room" appears in *Paterson
Literary Review* (Spring, 2020).

Cover by Mary Delaware

Paperback #13
A Jabber Publication, Chicago, Ill.
ISBN: 9781670847904

From Kan-yǔ 3, by Chen Zi'ang

The sun-bleached bones lie torn apart. . . .
Han soldiers, three hundred thousand of them,
Were once sent to confront the Hsiung-nu.
One sees only the dead on the battlefield,
Who would pity the widows and orphans by the border?

(Ho, trans., page 90)

List of Photo Illustrations

Du Fu's Thatched Cottage and Memorial Gardens, Chengdu

After the Polar Vortex

Shoveled the driveway clean
final double check
     visa application
     supporting documents
     passport
off to bed, asleep as I hit the pillow—
        wake late out the door
bare knuckles on icy roads
     to the train, the train

ah
in my seat soft breath soft light
no destination
     only wait
        & ride

                                  ⏀

Strange, taking in familiar streets & woods
from upper deck window in the dark—
now
freight yards, acres of junked cars
     snow-covered, hoods up
& beyond,
streets whose rhythms I've known intimately,
barely visible
         headlights unseen drivers
bare-knuckles on wheel
tense, struggling in snow piles & shiny
     layers of ice
here
traffic light signaling the road to home,

Suzy asleep in her bed
                    still,
Will laboring over
the rising action of his second novel
        one light still on over his computer.

                                        ⏃

On to Holland, where the train will fill, then
to Chicago
consulate on Erie Street, now
blasting thru the dark.
                            I dream of Beijing,
Chengdu where Du Fu built his thatched refuge,
found brief respite from endless war
        in bright mornings, garden and quiet evenings
driven out by yet another revolt, another invasion—
even as I roll across the yet unknown
landscapes / skyscapes to Suining,
home of Guan Yin and Chen Zi'ang.

                                        ⏃

May I make this journey with dignity and grace,
may I honor my poems and the poems of friends,
        make new friends, sing & laugh together.
Let me honor the spirit of my nation and my people,
sit humbly in the halls and gardens of ancient China,
        honor her people and her ancestors.
Let us enter a whole new world with open eyes & ears,
a clear heart, as father Whitman once did.

                                        ⏃

First streak of deep red along the horizon,
        below deep whitish blue billows

echoing deep blue-white of snowy fields,
one farmhouse light
almost at the horizon. White woods
in the valley below,
rising to hills above, now a great pond icy sheet
rimmed with brush, what spirits
must be waking here
to struggle through another day?
What eyes watch us pass,
even in the depths of deep forest
or in the workers' paradise kitchen window?
Jet passes overhead, sleepers
headed who knows where?
What wranglings, desires, dreams
& great extended conversations,
notes tapped out with tenuous fingers,
far above us here?

Chen Zi'ang and Du Fu

This was the final of four attempts to articulate my sense of the works and difficulties of Chen Zi'ang and Du Fu, two poets whom I knew would be important presences on this trip. Source for Chen Zi'ang stanza is "Taking Leave of Friends on a Night in Spring" (Ho, pages 145-146); source for Du Fu stanza is the Cheng Tu sequence (Hinton 53-71) and bio note (125-129), especially the lines "After ten desperate, headlong years, driven / perch to perch, I cling to what peace one twig holds" ("Overnight at Headquarters," Hinton 69).

The Moon

tonight, the full moon lights the snowy forest,
still blue dream beyond hope, beyond sorrow.

his memorials for harmony ignored again and again,
Chen spent a night with an old friend talking
mountains and streams, his coming journey to Loyang,
this night's deep bonds memorials to one he might
never see again—the road leading forever away—

Du Fu found a dream refuge in his thatched hut,
despite poverty, free of slavish work, among family
and friends—yet endless wars and rebellions
drove him off, clinging to a single twig, only
moonlight over waters shaped his long journey.

Thur. Feb 7

Leaving in the dark:
breezes shake ice crystals
from the white pine's branches—
shattering on frozen snow,
wild rhythms shaking the sleeper
    awake.

Tue Feb 26: Journey to Suining Begins.

Pere Marquette train to Chicago 5:45 a.m.
Took my first malaria pill with toast, yogurt, Boost protein drink @ 4:30—
no ill effects so far. Still musing on whether I can get help from Suining
folk re hotel & taxi to Du Fu Memorial in Chengdu 12 minutes from
airport—photos of it superb. Will have to rely on my new phone for
photos—camera has gone walkabout at last minute—no luck finding
it after multiple searches through luggage and house itself. So, be
satisfied.

Ah, to be leaving my home, family and cats, to go halfway around the
world for my poesy—whoda thunk I'd ever do this at age 71 when as an
angry kid I first fell in love with words—Emerson "snowstorm," Dylan
Thomas, falling for Latin & French, dreaming of other worlds I never
thought I'd see.

At Jane's place in Edgewater: lovely Greek meal brought to us by Andy's.
Arranged hotel room for March 6-7 at Hilton Chengdu (single, king bed,
non-smoking). We laughed and talked & Jane and I watched 3 episodes

5

of *Mrs. Maisel* before turning in.

5 a.m. Beijing current temp 53 degrees. Shedding 1 pr. pants, heavy sweater, scarf until return. Glucose reading: 112. When Jane gets up: go for coffee, then finish packing & take Lyft for O'Hare: need to scan passport + China visa to get boarding pass.

In flight: 2:30 p.m. Chicago time. I was, of course, aware that we'd be crossing the international date line, but did not know at this point that the flight would be heading north and turning west only when it reached the Arctic Sea. Under the roar of the engines, jibber-jabber of many voices, a kind of music as I write this, I turn to Du Fu's Chengdu poems. I've been through two more document checks (passport & visa) and filled out another form declaring my intentions (departure card/arrival card> necessary if I'm to be allowed to deplane). Dreaming of my hotel room in Beijing after end of this 13 hr. flight:

> "A perched bird knows the ancient Dao. Sails
> Only drift toward night in whose home?"
>   —Du Fu (Hinton, trans., page 71)

4:30 p.m. Chicago time: 3 ½ hours in air @ 550 mph—1850-1900 miles beyond Chicago—are we over the ocean? Dunno—United shut all the plane windows and turned off the lights. Same yakking going on behind me and to the right—Coleridge was famed as conversationalist, but these three make him out like a close-lipped piker.

Wonder what Sue and Will are doing now in our serene little living room? Cut off from the world here—phone in airplane mode / no wi-fi anyways.

Maybe hotel wi-fi for me in Beijing—then send love to friends and family.

Feb. 28

6:30 pm Chicago time. Six rows to my left, a passenger has opened her window, to spectacular rich red sky—she snaps photo after photo with her cell phone, an immensely beautiful dawn.

7:00 pm Chicago time: NW over Canada, we turned west at "Santa's workshop" (flight attendant's words) and are flying north of / parallel to Alaska's north coast. We'll turn south over Russian Siberia and fly straight to Beijing. Current time to destination: 6:50. Distance traveled so far: 3175 miles. Altitude: 36,000 feet [varies up to 39,000]. Outside air temp.: -71 degrees Fahrenheit.

11:00 pm Chicago time: miles covered this trip: 6686. Passage through Beijing airport lines was fairly swift, though I was lost as to how to get to taxi pickup— my hotel's shuttle service would not function for 2 ½ hours and after this long flight, I wanted to get to my room. I must have looked quite lost, because a young airport policewoman came up and walked me through the corridors 3/8 of a mile to the place where I'd catch the airport train, the taxi pickup area beyond the last stop. I thanked her and bowed slightly, then found my way. Two taxi drivers refused to take me to the hotel, and an airport official ordered the second one to take me. He was none too pleased, but took me on, and though I think he may have over-charged me, I was just glad to get there. Found my hotel room, hit the sack, took my blood glucose reading: 148 (yikes! Must be that airplane food!) and crashed.

March 1

< Blood glucose, 5 a.m. March 1: 102. Up at 6 a.m. Beijing time for
complimentary breakfast, in time to catch 7 a.m. shuttle to Air China /
terminal 3 for flight to Chengdu.

Waiting for dawn in Beijing hotel room—a memory
from the day before:
Capitol airport lines
         like JFK's though more quiet, orderly—
helpful airport cop showed me how to find taxi exit,
taking airport shuttle train to the end of the line—
         thinking of Du Fu, his many regrets & melancholy
as invaders closed in on his thatched sanctuary, though he
was still able to find the silences.
         We all have regrets, rethinking earlier choices,
                  behaviors,
as we age, yet there is a meditative space for those
limping toward death,
a quiet dance with each moment, and I despite myself
am giddy as a schoolboy in love
to be opening my eyes to a nation of great landscapes,
a people moving quickly into this century,
kids full of life, a young mother who'd talked with me
in Chicago as we waited for our plane,
the concerns for one's child in these early years,
bringing her teething child aboard a 13 hour flight
alone, pleased to be heard.

                  ☐

THIS WATER SHOULD BE BOILED BEFORE CONSUMING
         (handy large electric teapot near TV in my room).

News: Trump admits "sometimes you've just got to walk away" after failure of Kim summit. (waiting for the spin & blame game).

To Chengdu from Beijing: shuttle from hotel to airport Terminal 3 (Air China) > 4th floor > get in "Foreigners" line to get into Air China area > K > get help with boarding pass, then get coffee (Lei Café). On to Chinese check on my bags etc.—most thorough pat-down I've ever had (all but crotch)—usual stuff through screening, but I had to pull all medicines/soaps etc. out to run through screener a second time. I was thankful—more assurance that I'd be flying in safety

12:30. Lunch of Chinese cuisine, better than United—beef & mushrooms, veggies, clear noodles w. mushrooms, and the peculiar yet lovely soupy yogurt with somewhat higher sugar content than my Skyr. 3 cups of green tea! Another hour & 15 mins. on this flight—anxious to meet Suining folk at the airport and hopeful for the 148 km drive to the city—according to Jim Ruggia, the loveliest mountains and valleys, winding streams which should stir my romantic heart borne of my beginnings with Wordsworth ("the stolen boat," etc.), Keats, & strangely enough, Emerson & Thoreau, but of course mostly an echo of my childhood along the Thornapple River, with that waterway a world in my canoe, paths up over the tops of moraines leading who knew where until you went. Excited to see some Chinese rivers, mountains and valleys and meet new friends.

On the road, I recall the crazy German I met on the shuttle headed to Beijing airport, who inquired re. my reasons for going to Chengdu—one thing led to another, and before long he was searching out my online

papers at U of Michigan Special Collections Library, asking about my career
and the publishing industry—we rattled on between that and Kurosawa's
Ran and other classic adaptations of Shakespeare, then questions of China
and hotels and collaborative management, my old man's specialty back in
his work days—and suddenly we were at the airport, helped each other find
directions to our respective gates. He described himself as an industrial slave
caught in the machine despite good money—but I could see his mind was
agile and would serve him well once he got free of the meat grinder. Pause
here to consider the many great Chinese poets who longed to free themselves
of court and attaché pencil-pushing work, searching for refuge from conniving
officials, murderous plots, being trapped in military expeditions—always with a
hope of going to the country and living quietly. Du Fu tried, Chen Zi'ang and
Li Bai lamented the patterns of their lives even as they struggled to find inner
peace, not so different from middle management folks in our age, though the
stakes were higher for many of the T'ang poets who also served through much
of their lives as administrative officials.

Chengdu by Air: A Meditation

Shuangliu International Airport was founded as a military airport for the
Republic of China's defense against the Japanese assault on China beginning
in 1937, with deliberate aerial bombing of civilian targets. Chinese pilots paid
with their lives in the battles against the superior Japanese planes, but the US
Army Air Force joined them in 1942, bringing their P-38 Lightnings and P-47
fighter-bombers to drive the Japanese from the air. I pondered the fact that I
would be flying into an airport that had been a major base for the liberation
of China during that war, immediately thinking back to vivid and
uncomfortable childhood memories.

Friends whose fathers had fought in that war often mused over the war stories
their fathers had shared, but I was the kid whose dad did not see combat, and
thus was left with a sense of something missing. My dad had graduated from
Michigan as a metallurgical engineer in the fateful year of 1942, and eventually
found work helping with the design of weapons and vehicles. At the time, he
was deemed more suited to producing the materials that would make victory
possible against a ferocious enemy. I would understand his reticence about the
war much later, but at the time, I found myself as an awed listener, fascinated
and horrified by the books of war photos that one friend brought to school with
him. I particularly recall the photos of the Japanese dead, bloated almost
beyond recognition, with ripped flesh and gaping bullet holes in their bloody
clothing.

Later, I joined the boy scouts, and was quite proud of the fact that I had earned
merit badges in Nature and Indian Lore; eventually I would spend a year
memorizing passages from the Bible, visiting many different kinds of churches,
synagogues, etc., and doing long work in a church garden, raising tomatoes, corn

11

and other vegetables to sell to neighbors—raising money for those in need. Yet in our scout meetings, my fellow scouts discovered that our scout leader had been a fighter pilot in World War II, and they made themselves nuisances, pestering him for his war stories.

He was a good man, had taught us a remarkable amount about leadership, discipline, respect for the natural world and for other humans, and was plainly uncomfortable with their requests. Finally, after weeks of their badgering, he turned to us all, exasperated, and said, "OK, I will tell you this once, and after that, I never want to hear about this again." He paused a moment, and then in a plaintive voice said, "it is horrifying to drive your plane through the debris and body parts of a man whom you have just killed, to see the blood and flesh streaking your wind screen." My friends were stunned, and after a brief pause, he continued: *"now* do you get it?"

That thought has been with me all these years, and I brought up my scout leader's tale with my community college students when introducing them to Hemingway's *A Farewell to Arms* and his World War I Nick Adams stories, famed for close observation of what then was known as "shell shock," and now is understood as post-traumatic stress disorder. Ernest followed the effects of these wounds closely, detailing the mental and spiritual damage, and I knew that students who were Vietnam, Gulf War, Afghan War veterans and the victims of war in Bosnia and Africa would all be moved by this. My thought has always been to give students a space to explore experiences that keep them from reaching fulfillment in their lives, to "clear the decks" as it were, to find their way to intellectual and spiritual lives that can be productive, sane, and thoughtful enough to want to help others. Some *needed* to write about their experiences; I gave them instant permission to do so, and these students invariably produced work of enormous depth and awareness of what violence can do to each of us.

Others came to me sheepishly after class, needing to talk privately, and one came, asking to drop the class. I asked him if I was out of line teaching these stories, and he quickly responded, "No! No, I came back from the war and thought I had put it behind me, but then the stories here made me aware that I was still trapped in what I saw. I need to get counseling, and you've made me see what I need to do to get right." One Bosnian student even went so far as wanting to publish her story in the college's literary magazine; I asked if she would be troubled to know that thousands of others would be reading her story, and she looked up fiercely and said, "Americans *need* to know stories like this!"

All this went through my mind as I mused on the history of Chengdu's airport, and when I researched the city itself, I discovered that it is now a burgeoning center for travel to the west for research facilities as well as to the south, that it is a major business center with nine ring roads outside the main city center —a huge city plainly on the move. It occurred to me that, without the efforts of Chinese and American warriors in World War II, much of this might look very different now, and many now alive would never have been conceived. I thought, too, of Chen Zi'ang's horror over the price of war as seen in poems viewing the shattered bones of warriors and the intense grief of widows and children. Du Fu also came to mind—his retreat to Chengdu in the hope of finding respite from the murderous struggles of his time, and of being driven from his home by violent hordes after only a few years in his thatched cottage.

First Night in Suining

An amazing finale to my first night in Suining: a walk out to Shenglian Island (in the middle of the city) to a combined restaurant/art gallery devoted to Guan Yin and the famed lotuses that fill Guan Yin lake, which adjoins the island / also a pottery shop, all both rustic and sophisticated. A multicourse meal of the best Chinese dishes I've ever had up to this point, shared and hosted by Suining City cultural and tourism officials and our guides and interpreters, followed by a stroll and interpretive walk through the galleries, observing the sculpture (heads of Guan Yin predominate) and elegant bas relief dancers and musicians. Then night came on and the entire mile walk around the lake lit up with a lantern fair (see photos following the journal entry for this night), gigantic many-colored balloons or "lanterns" formed as temples, animals and flowers, human figures, all dominated by the enormous lit-up figure of Guan Yin pouring the water of mercy, kindness and compassion on the city (she is an icon of their hoped-for sensibility, and as I learned on the next day, the city holds two temple complexes and an ashram dedicated to her, the first on Wolong Mountain and bearing the distinction of being the oldest Buddhist temple in Western China, and the second dedicated to helping those in difficult circumstances, compassionate healing as the important key there).

Through the evening, I got to know two of my fellow international poet conferees, Russian poet Olesia Nikolaeva and Erik Lindner from Holland. Erik and I talked about Amsterdam and the Dutch penchant for compassion for the oppressed (e.g. Ann Frank), and I mentioned Joseph Brodsky at Michigan to Olesia, which brought up the dilemma of the Russian poet in the U. S.—thinking in one language and culture while writing in another. I mentioned Carmen Bugan's thesis on the poetry of exile, negotiating *living* in a new culture while thinking in one's own. Olesia wondered if Brodsky's writings in English were troubling for odd grammar and word choices, as many critics have claimed—I said, only to a grammar and vocabulary purist. The U. S. has one great language gift—many tongues, many voices and verbal structures borne of the languages and cultures of immigrants from across the globe as well as the place-naming gifts borne of Spanish and French colonists, and especially Native Americans, the continent's "first people"—and all are to be valued.

We also talked of Ken Rexroth's translations and of the big event in current Chinese critical appreciations of Gary Snyder (3 books!!), and of his part in our fashioning the Declaration of Interdependence at Naropa in 1990. Turns out that Olesia's husband knew Professor Proffer, the University of Michigan professor who journeyed to Europe and rescued Brodsky when he was exiled from the USSR, bringing him to Ann Arbor and helping him become an instructor there, a base to begin a new career and new life.

<Back to Conifer Hotel, take malaria pill, clean up, boil extra water for future needs (tap water must be boiled here, as in Beijing, before it can be ingested). Off to bed, sleeping four hours then waking to share some of this with Sue via phone message—thanks for the new phone, which makes this kind of communication possible when one has no internet. In the morning, we visit Guangde Temple, one of three dedicated to Guan Yin in China, two of which are located here in Suining. Satisfaction.

Wake at 5:44: blood glucose level: 97. Total of six hours of sleep, enough to sustain me for the strenuous day ahead.

Six of the many photos I took on this trip follow: two from the lantern festival previously described, and four from the Guangde Temple complex on Wolong Mountain (text for that journal entry follows the photos):

International Poets at Suining

Juan Carlos Mestre / Madrid, Spain
(winner of the International Poetry Award)

Alexandra Dominguez / Chile and Madrid, Spain

Renato Sandoval Bacigalupo / Peru

Maria Rosa Lojo / Argentina
(husband Oscar from Germany, an engineer)

Guillermo Bravo / Argentina, Italy

Javier Fernández / Spain embassy education adviser

Erik Lindner / Amsterdam, Holland

Olesia Nikolaeva / Russia

A J (Andy) Carruthers / Australia

Olga Vinogradova / Russia

Luciá Fernandez / Argentina

Jonathan (Jon) Morley / England

David Cope / Michigan, USA

March 2

After breakfast in the Conifer Hotel 2nd floor restaurant, spent the morning climbing through the various levels of the Guangde Temple complex with Erik, Olesia, a film and photography crew, and our guides, all this on Wolong Mountain beyond the central city, which lies below it. First, a welcome at the nearby city level entrance and short hike up to the first statue shrine, a 15-20 ft. tall golden statue of Guan Yin and her two sisters mounted on lotus base in plaza—three Suining women giving blessings to all, trees and bushes nearby thickly draped with red prayer flags.

Then, the first level temple complex with some parked cars, central gateway leading to a courtyard and square with monks and mostly elderly working class folk and some young families meditating together on zafus and awaiting a homily from the monk in charge. This is still a working temple, and we were cautioned not to take photos of services such as this one or of the statues inside the shrine buildings, both of which are sacred services that demand respect and attentiveness for the ceremonial moment. All this reminded me of similar scenes at Naropa Institute (now University) in the 1980s, though here these services have gone on for 1300 years and more, and there's a kind of *knowing* borne of these traditions that is in the very atmosphere here—this quite different from the services at Naropa, where the sangha was just forming, still amorphous and perhaps anxious to establish itself. These old people have their faith in their bones and in generations of ancestors, and one can see it in their eyes.

We ascended to the next level of buildings—all constructed on the same principles of construction employed in the Forbidden City—elements of the design balanced via the physics of counterpressure and locking parts, without nails or screws, more flexible in earthquake zones. Lovely golden gabled ends with animals periodically and in some ways whimsically enhancing the architecture (with the inevitable dragons usually among them), nearby mountain tops visible in openings beyond the roofs.

Further upwards, an open pagoda near three sacred wells, each connected to a different underground river source far below—the three echoing the three sisters, Guan Yin and her siblings. Hike upward on road reveals stele for monks who innovated Buddhist practice over hundreds of years of discipline, then along the ascending walkway a stone dragon head neatly carved and above that a wall with a dragon body all along it—decorated with diplodocus and apatosaurus riding along its sides.

Yet another plateau with enormous complex of temple buildings topped by large pagoda, three arches joined atop huge flight of stairs as entryway to that level. More stairs, and at the next plateau, the whole city of Suining spread below in the distance. Here one climbs another set of stairs with enormous writhing stone dragon bodies in bas relief, contained in a center section between the two sets of stairs, giant pagoda atop that with roofs of the lower section splayed out before us. Climbing up the stairways to different levels around this building, more and more is revealed on the exterior walkways— this is the shrine of the golden gigantic Guan Yin, where you can drink from the sacred well, pray on zafus and if you so choose, "have your wishes granted." I donated 50 yuan, prayed for the peace of those in need, and kept moving. Eventually, Erik and I ascended to the top step of this highest shrine, an enormous task all told—the entire hike took a full three hours, all of this time allowing our minds to settle and wander freely in a dream of clarity and the notion of kindness.

Camera crew had interviewed Erik further down (the first of many interviews for us all), and now on the very heights they came at me. Two questions: first, the importance of Guan Yin to me—they and others had noticed from day one that I was knowledgeable and committed to her—this one the easiest to answer: "she represents all the qualities most lacking and most in need in today's world—compassion, kindness, and mercy." Second, what could Suining do to enhance and combine the gifts of its two most famed citizens (Guan Yin and Chen Zi'ang)?

I suggested that each kind of wisdom is incomplete in and of itself—poets bring eloquence and clarity to language, but without some kind of spiritual grounding, the mind can grow self-important and partial. Buddhists can lose sight of the clarity of their calling without language precision—each can help the other, as Chogyam Trungpa announced when forming the poetics school at Naropa Institute. Chen Zi'ang is particularly important: his memoranda to the empress unfailingly but politely insisted on harmonious actions as the means to create harmony in government; he had courage at a time when many were losing their heads among the court elite, and hundreds of thousands of peasant soldiers were being butchered in war: see his Kan-yǔ poems #3 and #37, the latter of which ends, "I heave a loud sigh, whom do I lament? The people on the frontier, for the grass is soaked with their blood" (Ho, pages 90, 126). Also, he is now recognized as the innovator in poetry among those in the T'ang Dynasty—the one who stripped away the obfuscating symbolism, folderol, and the insinuating sensuality that had infected court poetry for over a hundred years—he insisted on seeing the world as it is and that language should open up the possibilities in one's thoughts, not shade things in unnaturally forced approaches to content. He provides a path through his poems which rewards clarity and precision.

I should point out that, in the poems, he sometimes employs subject matter from earlier times to invisibly comment on current events, employing the "indirect speech" that subtly speaks of forbidden issues through a kind of allegory—a practice common in all nations where tyranny is rebuked for those who read "between the lines." Shakespeare and Ben Jonson employed this method under the reigns of Elizabeth I and James I, especially in their Roman plays.

Back at Conifer Hotel, we meet German engineer Oscar and his Argentinian poet wife Maria, plus Olga Vinogradova (Russian)—all just arrived for the conference—and two Chinese poets who have come to give blessings on our lunch.

March 3

The previous day's experiences gave me the grist to begin drafting the poem that each of us had been asked to produce as emblematic of our thoughts on Suining and the week we'd spend here. I woke at 4:00 a.m. and wrote the first draft of "From the Top Step of Guangde Temple," a poem that went through four drafts before breakfast three hours later. Last year, I was on tour promoting my new and selected poems, *The Invisible Keys*, also completing selection of those poems I wanted for a Collected Poems—yet I also knew that this book would not be complete until I finish the final group of meditations borne of aging and finding comfort in my coming death. I had already completed two poems in this sequence, but I also have been deeply aware that bringing those poems into focus from each period of my life has been a trial borne of the hope that the changed circumstances of my life and the world beyond would produce poems that would be substantially different from those that preceded them. This poem and the others that come from my experiences of China, her history and her poets, involves a struggle with myself, with the poets and the great saintly figure of Guan Yin, with almost continuous meditations on *their* lives and wisdom, all while honing a sense of how to capture the city and landscapes as I experience them in the light of the long history they embody.

Sichuan Song Dynasty Porcelain Museum: A National Treasure

Of the many photos I took at the Ceramic Museum, I chose the four examples following this journal entry as illustrations of the grace and beauty of these treasured works of art from the Song Dynasty (960-1279). The Museum narrator explained that "the work here is Longquan celadon unearthed from the Jinyucun cache, blue as sunset sky, not showy nor meretricious." The greater elaboration of the kinds of ceramic vessels available during this period go hand-in-hand with the development of tea culture and ceremonies and with the rise of the brewing industry, resulting in a need for new kinds of works to transport and to drink alcoholic drinks. "Brewing led to enabling people to drink together—grog shops spread all over the area, the drinking shared by all social classes."

After the Ceramic Museum, we visited the second Guan Yin temple complex, this one down in the city and administering to people in difficult circumstances and in need of healing. It also featured the famous white jade Buddha and a tall stupa containing the relics of a saintly monk. I took a lot of photos at this complex, but I have not reproduced them here.

March 4

Blood glucose reading: 97.

We have been heavily covered by the press and by TV interviews. There were at least three articles on the conference, with numerous interviews, film crews tracking us everywhere, and groups of still photographers. This was sometimes distracting, particularly for the members of the sanghas who'd come to experience sacred worship, but it also sometimes interfered with my own concentration on the experiences we were being shown—quite unlike my public work at home in the U. S., where we are generally lucky to have a few reporters show up for a reading or event. Next, we visit Chen Zi'ang Reading House, site of his childhood home in Shehong, on a tall hill over the local river. We read one poem each to the gathered conferees, scholars, et. al., and I found myself besieged by reporters wanting interviews, which was pleasant though caused me to miss several readings that I wanted to hear. I do recall one of these interviews: a young reporter wanted me to speak of the kinds of poetry we can write in the U. S., and I mentioned at length that we are "wide open," and a poet can choose one or more of an enormous variety of approaches to the writing of poems, mentioning several—A J Carruthers, in his chanted message on the 5th, gave a rousing litany of the many approaches to composition available in the West, much more comprehensive than I could summon for this reporter today. While waiting to read my 9-11 poem, "In Silence," a young associate professor of comparative literature at Peking University, Qin Liyan, sought me out, and we had a fairly involved discussion of Chen's work, his Kan-yǔ #3—the battleground with shattered bones poem—resembling a scene in Dante, which she immediately noted must be the scene associated with Farinata in *Inferno*. I was impressed.

March 4: Silence and Ten Thousand People's Poem Party at Shehong

The gigantic statue of Chen Zi'ang promised sensitive, clear-eyed poetry that would not flinch from a quiet demand for harmony, and the grief felt by the poet when witnessing the thousands of shattered skeletons on a battlefield, his sense of pain in the hearts of widows and orphans. The gathering crowds were promising, too, and we poets wondered what this event would involve, who would perform their poems, and if those gifted with words could honor the spirit of the poet whose iconic presence stood before us.

As it turned out, this event involved fourteen carefully choreographed narrative dance sequences performed expertly by elementary and middle school students, with music so loud and chants shouted in an ear-splitting monotone—and, to top it off, drones flying roughly ten feet over our heads, their engines loud enough to be distracting while simultaneously blowing cold air down directly upon us. The entire event was organized by municipal and county officials, and while *Poetry Periodical* and the Sichuan Writers Association were listed among the sponsors, I had a feeling that they didn't have much input on the selection of works to be presented. There was certainly a fine set of school presentations for the benefit of friends, family, and the city of Shehong, but there was no poetry at this event. My ears were in pain at the end of this set of performances, but it also had me reflecting on the nature of poetry, especially the art's insistence on absolute rhythm underlining the emotional tenor of each line, and on subtlety in execution, with an awareness of the power of silence. I reflected long and hard on this, and having had time to think further about it, I turn to the approaches taken by poets whose work fills me with utmost respect.

Barry Miles' recent essay, "The Beat Goes On: A Century of Lawrence

Ferlinghetti," notes the poet's insistence on the importance of silence in the making of the poem: his style has been based on "open form," a term derived from nonobjective painting and used by poets Robert Duncan and Charles Olson. "The basis of my typography, the Open Form typography, was if there's a word isolated by itself on a page, white space is silence." Similarly, in poems such as "For Eleanor and Bill Monahan," William Carlos Williams described his sense of counting a beat for each line, long or short, in terms of the time involved—thus presuming a space of silence with the short line (See his letter to Richard Eberhart on May 13, 1954, in *The Selected Letters of William Carlos Williams*, pages 326-327).

In those poems of mine that depart from "standard" typography, I have followed their approach to sound and silence, finding that unusual silences between words and phrases can give the listener a meditative space or a moment of emphasis within the poem—important, I think, in that poetry should be an art that not only sings the quiet music of the syllables within lines, but also finds their moments of emotional punctuation, as in Pound's notion of "absolute rhythm." One thinks of the two heavy spondees that open each of the first three lines of *Inferno* III, hammers that could echo the heavy beating of the fearful heart. Such skillful artistry is the grist of great poems, which are carefully constructed to present a piece that opens spaces and selects the variations in spoken rhythms befitting the emotional tenor of the line. The emphasis is often, too, in the subtlety of the variations.

March 5 (Jane's birthday)

Blood glucose reading: 124   4 a.m.

Today: Planning travel March 6-8: I started by laying this itinerary out clearly so that I'd have a sense of what the schedules were for the next three days:

March 6: Depart Suining with Dr. Zhao and Spanish poets 7:30 a.m.

Itinerary: visit Panda Research Center and Du Fu's Memorial Garden, then drop off poets at airport and check in at Hilton Chengdu after 3 p.m.

Other concerns: as we started, Dr. Zhao Si laid out the itinerary and timing of our trip so that connections and arrival times would be clear to us, calming my concerns about "how I'd get where."

At hotel: ask about morning airport shuttle in a.m. so that I may arrive in plenty of time to find my way to my flight to Beijing.

March 7: Flight to Beijing
Shuttle or taxi to airport no later than noon (11 a.m. preferred).
Air China terminal.
Flight CA 4103 to Beijing 2-4:30.
Taxi (or shuttle, beginning at 6:30) to Holiday Inn Beijing Airport Zone

March 8: Departure to airport and flight to Chicago
latest shuttle possible (up to 9 or 10 a.m.) to United Airlines International at Beijing Capitol Airport
THANKS FOR AIRPORT SHUTTLE DRIVER> terminal 3, not 2.
UA 850 12:15 p.m. to Chicago
Arr. March 9 11:15 a.m. Sat.

March 5: Dialogue between International and Chinese Poets
on the Greater Issues of Poetry Today

This session begins with copious amounts of excellent green tea, the distribution of earphones and speakers, and the gift of a 283 page book featuring all of the poet conferees, most with their photographs and bios and all with at least one of their poems. Script is all in Chinese; I asked for and received a second copy for my archive at U of Michigan, with thanks that I wanted the conference materials preserved in a U. S. university in this way. This day's work is the central event of the entire week: a day of direct cross-cultural dialogue of global import for the future of poetry. We were all outfitted with earphones and speakers who translated whatever language was being spoken into our own tongues—"a regular United Nations of Poetry."

The editor-in-chief of *Poetry Periodical* began the session by posing a question: could the international poets make suggestions that might help contemporary Chinese poets prepare to take their place among the poets of the international community as fully involved with contemporary practice and issues? This question "set my hair on fire," and I departed from my prepared essay to make suggestions involving equality and full representation of women, minorities and others in Chinese works. I noted that this move involved both risks and rewards, especially as those who have been underrepresented may have experiences not commensurate with those who are presently privileged—and "equality" presumes the right to share such life events as exclusion, oppression, and struggle to be given dignity.

Other international poets came up with their own thoughts on the matter, perhaps the most memorable for me being Australian A. J. Carruthers, whose chant naming the many experiments with style and form rose to a fever pitch as he emphasized points of endless experimentation in the art of "making it new." The Chinese poets responded in the afternoon, some suggesting that the established forms were central to Chinese poetry, and that it would not be wise to deviate too far from them, while two poets believed that despite China's newfound wealth and progressive move into 21st century technologies, many younger poets are full of anxiety about their future, some even contemplating suicide: old forms cannot suffice for these poets, who want to find new ways of articulating their own experiences. This honesty was heartening to me; while I highly value the old poetics of our own classic writers, I have always seen them as teachers of technique and sound that can find a new home augmenting current approaches to the art. Perhaps the greatest surprise came with the testimony of an elder Mongolian poet, who felt that too much emphasis on technique or form misses the point: Chinese poets need to develop *empathy*, he said, telling the story of an older woman worker whose boss did not provide her with adequate equipment to do her job. This woman fell from a defective ladder and died as a result, and there was no one to repeat the story, to grieve over the loss to friends, family and co-workers. The poet noted too that when he has tried to submit poems of this caliber to publications, editors invariably dismissed his work out of hand, as though such subject matter is beneath them. I was moved by his testimony, and with Ray (my guide) translating, I thanked him for touching on a subject that has been central in my own work, and naturally it gave me pause to consider a poetics that engaged the themes central to Guan Yin herself, as well to the work of Chen Zi'ang.

The entire question haunted me through the rest of the conference and beyond, especially when I considered how I first found my way to Dante,

Villon, Virgil, Horace, Catullus, and such modern greats as Lorca, Neruda, Akhmatova, Brodsky, Rilke, and others. The path was always through translations, except in the case where one has learned the language or learned to "hear" a word in the original through its analogue in a language from the same "family"—grasping a word or phrase in Dante's Italian, for example, through analogue soundings in Latin, French or Spanish. When one has no recourse to language study, the translations *must do* unless one can be present at a dual reading in both languages, or hear recordings of the original with script and translation. I naturally thought that contemporary Chinese poets need to be known first through skilled translations, as Wang Ping did when she first came to the United States, editing a complete collection of then-younger Chinese poets in translation in *New Generation: Poems from China Today* (Hanging Loose Press, 1999). It is also important that the contemporary Chinese poets find their way into the publishing streams of other nations, as international poets at this conference have done in being published and known in China. I thought, too, of the struggles that Professor Zhang and I went through when a word or phrase in my poem just could not be translated properly into Chinese, and the two of us fumbled around with this problem via email exchanges until we came up with a solution that satisfied us both; I knew that *skilled* translation between two quite dissimilar languages would require careful and sustained dialogue on the parts of everyone involved in the project: bridges such as these should be built to last.

Thoughts borne of the initial question and the responses of participants, or on the question of building language bridges between us popped up in emails and in conversations throughout the weeks after I returned home, and it would seem that a conference on the art of translation would be in order. Given that the need of a shared language base is imperative, translations would initially fulfill the need to make contemporary Chinese poets' work available first in the languages of nations where they need to be heard—a necessary first step to recognition by poets in another culture, even if not in the language and sound of the originals. Ultimately, it would be good for universities both in China and elsewhere to train advanced students in the art of translation, to accelerate this first stage of recognition, and to make the magazine and anthology publishers of those nations aware that these poets are looking for a reading of their work. Perhaps in time, enough younger poets in other nations will learn the Chinese language, poetic masters, traditions, and innovations so that they will be able to hear the sound of the originals as they read them.

☒

After this session, I was fairly exhausted and, having a big travel day ahead tomorrow, ate dinner, skipped the evening Opera performance and went back to my hotel room, cleaning up and ordering my things for rapid early morning departure. See my earlier plans for March 6, pages 39).

I have looked forward to the visit to Du Fu's "thatched cottage" and extensive memorial garden ever since I read about it in Bill Porter's unparalleled travelogue / critical appreciation and translation / homage to China's great poets of earlier times, *Finding Them Gone: Visiting China's Poets of the Past* (Copper Canyon, 2016).

I had always enjoyed Du Fu's poems, teaching a few of them in my creative writing classes, but during those busy years I never had occasion to do an in-depth study of his life and work. Now was the time, and after exploring the biographical materials at the end of David Hinton's translations of the selected poems, I carefully worked my way through the poems twice, then centered on the Chengtu (Chengdu) poems so that I could connect them on a deeper level with the place of refuge that he intended his thatched cottage to be.

It was thus with a deep hunger that this trip would lead to real satisfaction in walking on the grounds and musing over the life of China's greatest poet. We had to, of course, visit Panda Base first, as others wanted to see the pandas, so I figured I'd take photos there for children at home (I had seen pandas before—in Washington), and wait for my time with the great poet's memory. Photos follow.

March 6, After Visiting Du Fu's Garden

Arrived at hotel in a timely fashion, my comrades departing from Du Fu's garden in a separate car, headed for airport. Settled in, selected a fine restaurant in the hotel, and treated myself with a superb filet mignon dinner with coffee and milk, a reward for this incredibly meaningful week.

March 7

Blood glucose reading: 104   4:45 a.m.

This morning, while waiting for complimentary breakfast area to open, I reflected back on the week, certainly one of those I'll remember as a life changer, though there were four distinct highlights and a set of relationships I hope I can continue later. The four highlights were: visiting Guangde Temple Complex and climbing three hours, all the way to the top step, thankful; reading "In Silence" in Chen Zi'ang's childhood back yard to the assembled conferees, and musing that this was his place of beginning; attending and participating on the great all day international poetry symposium on March 5, and being able to wander for hours through Du Fu's home ground during his years in Chengdu, getting a greater understanding of the importance of poetry in the long history of China's ancient heritage.

Hotel shuttle takes me to Chengdu Airport, where I board my plane for Beijing, sigh, arrive at Capitol Airport and have to wait a few hours for the Holiday Inn shuttle to start up again. When he finally arrives, he dilly-dallies around waiting for an acquaintance who was apparently working at the airport, and I get to my hotel at around 8:30 p.m. as a result. I arrange early shuttle to Capitol airport, knowing that I'll likely have some snafus in finding my way to the proper gate. To bed.

March 8 / Beijing

Blood glucose: 108   4:15 a.m.

Some key recollection of Ginsberg essay documentation in Hu Liang's book, which he gave me at the symposium. Again, it would be useful to have translation of the essay so that I could fully understand its import. Yet he does cite the following:

> Bill Morgan (Beat Generation, Deliberate Prose): 13, 16
> Kerouac (Dharma Bums): 14
> Allen (America, Kaddish): 15
> Bob Rosenthal: 15
> Burroughs (Naked Lunch): 18
> Andre Gide: 19
> Blake: 20
> Allen (Peyote, Moloch, The Bathers): 20
> Ken Kesey (One Flew Over etc): 21
> Allen (The Change): 22
> Rimbaud: 23
> Dylan: 23
> Neal Cassady: 23
> Joan Anderson letter: 24
> WCW: 24, 25
> Kerouac (Some of the Dharma): 26
> Raymond Weaver: 26
> Whitman: 26
> Rexroth: 27
> Snyder: 27
> McClure: 27
> Schumacher (Lion of Dharma): 29

Allen (One Morning I took a Walk
in China, Reading Bai Juyi): 30
Bob Rosenthal: 32
"Post-Beat, Neo-Beat": 32
Donald Lev: 32
Jack Foley: 33
Vernon Fraser: 33

Also, I checked Zhang's translations of my work and found that "The Storm" is the translation chosen to represent my work in the anthology of conference participants.

On to the airport, another long flight, this one to Chicago, hoping to see Jane as soon as she gets home.

March 8 / Chicago

Arrive at O'Hare early, quick run through customs, catch a taxi and arrive at Jane's place, call upstairs—Bryce comes down to let me in, and tired, I go to sleep. Jane and Bea come home after 2-3 hours and we order Indian food (palek paneer for me, YUM!) which I pay for gladly, enjoying my daughter's company among her friends.

March 9

In the morning, we all go up to Greek restaurant and share a breakfast, then Jane and I go to Gethsemane Gardens to buy gifts for family, she lines me up with a Lyft to Union Station, and I'm homeward bound. Returning from a

Florida vacation, my sister-in-law Cathy joins me, and we alternately share travel stories, laugh a bit, and occasionally doze off. Home by 11:30, still amazed I made this great journey and everything clicked despite all the potential troubles. Today, I am thankful and this journal dutifully reports the tale, both the important and exciting parts, and the mundane details.

David Cope

Entered on 21-25 March 2019 / Revised 26 and 28 March, 21-23 April 2019,
12-19 May 2019, June 6-10, June 16 (thanks to Jim Cohn for editing notes on June 15)

From the Top Step of Guangde Temple

Suining rests in its lotus cradle of wetlands,
conifers, blue mountains beyond mountains,

Guan Yin's poured waters in streams & passing
clouds, a stillness for the beating heart.

Chen Zi'ang saw the shattered bones of warriors,
sorrows of court & commoners, stood fast

for harmony, wept at the losses & sought refuge.
now, a grizzled old man scratches his head

on the bridge over Fujian River, traffic races
the changing lights, horns frantic & restless.

yet at the shrine, a small boy helps his grandpa
lift a frail leg over the high doorway,

poets drink from the sacred well as an aged monk
hammers the gong, echoing through the centuries.

Afterword:
Warfare and Violence, Poetry and Unacknowledged Legislators

The discovery of Chen Zi'ang's compassionate political activism, his honesty and clear vision re the brutality of war and empathy for its living victims has inspired me. Here was a poet who fearlessly spoke truth to power while reshaping the values of poetry in the T'ang. His work also led to meditations on my own life and that of my American contemporaries.

Perhaps it was the memories of sufferers and mangled dead among my parents' generation, or possibly those who died horribly in Vietnam or came home to a torturous life-in-death punishment played out in their minds or in obsessive PTSD behaviors. It may be in the endless litany of violent mass murders in American schools, pubs, churches, temples, mosques, public squares, movie houses—or in the police violence against black and brown men, road rage shootings or drug-deals-gone-wrong; regardless, my work in poetry and in political advocacy involves a major thread of empathy for those who suffer and exposes this massive problem that lives like a cancer in the very heart of what we fondly call "civilization."

Thus, at the Chen Zi'ang awards ceremony, when one of the children's dance sequences lit up in fire with a militaristic paean to armed conflict, I was to say the least troubled as I made my way back to my hotel room later. In the Shehong ceremonies, I was again troubled by the enactment of the Long March with its prominent display of automatic weapon props, as I am every year by my own nation's Fourth of July ceremonies. On reflecting further, I thought of how most nations display their veterans as national heroes in militaristic celebrations, neglecting their roles as victims of conflict and obfuscating the criminal complicity of corporations, politicians and arms

manufacturers amid the flag-waving pomp and circumstance. The illusions
are presented as truths before Agincourt:

> He that shall see this day and live to old age,
> Will yearly on the vigil feast his neighbors,
> And say, "Tomorrow is Saint Crispian."
>
> Then will he strip his sleeve and show his scars,
> And say, "These wounds I had on Crispin's day."
> . . .
> This story shall the good man teach his son,
> And Crispin Crispian shall ne'er go by
> From this day to the ending of the world,
> But we in it shall be remembered;
> We few, we happy few, we band of brothers.
>
> (Shakespeare, H5 4.3.46-50, 58-62)

I recalled my distaste for the U. S. national holiday, in which every city and
country town displays its veterans, fires off simulated bombs and fireworks
into the night in imitation of the "rockets' red glare, the bombs bursting in
air" from the drinking song that became our national anthem. Thomas
Jefferson, our third president, came to mind: "the tree of liberty must be
refreshed from time to time with the blood of patriots and tyrants"
(Jefferson 166). I've thought long and hard about how my nation is immersed
in a culture of violence, not only in the already-noted gun violence and
nearly continuous warfare that we engage in, but in the violent television
shows, games, films that reinforce it, and in the NRA's grasping influence
on legislators. My own work focuses on victims, those forgotten in the public
need to celebrate heroes and damn villains.

Still, poetry and literature *have* played their part in valorizing the horrors of war as normative behaviors, beginning with the *Iliad* and in biblical justifications for the slaughter of enemies, as with the women singing that "Saul has killed thousands, and David tens of thousands," or in the destruction of cities from Jericho to Sodom, and in the frenzied fantasy of the predicted apocalypse of *Revelation*. Simone Weil has explored the theme eloquently in her famed essay, "*The Iliad*, or the Poem of Force":

> The true hero, the true subject matter, the center of the *Iliad*
> is force. The force that men wield, the force that subdues men,
> in the face of which human flesh shrinks back. The human
> soul seems ever conditioned by its ties with force, swept
> away, blinded by the force it believes it can control, bowed un-
> der the constraint of the force it submits to. . . . Force is that
> which makes a thing of whoever submits to it. Exercised
> to the extreme, it makes the human being a thing quite liter-
> ally, that is, a dead body. . . . As pitilessly as force annihilates,
> equally without pity it intoxicates those who possess or be-
> lieve they possess it. (Weil 45, 51)

Those involved with a national or tribal agenda may easily ascribe a claim like this to those whom they identify as enemies, yet find it extremely difficult to confront the darkness at the center of our nature as humans: "turn the searchlight inward," as Gandhi once said. It is also a "memorable fancy" to believe with Shelley that poets are the "unacknowledged legislators of the world," yet such a claim partakes of hopeful illusion. Most nations also have a long history of literature that exposes, denounces, attempts to transcend the horrors of war as in the Old Testament *Lamentations*, the plays of Aristophanes, Aeschylus and Euripides.

Closer to our time, poems such as Emerson's "Ode Inscribed to William H. Channing," Whitman's compassionate Civil War nursing of maimed and dying soldiers (and eventual withdrawal due to likely PTSD) in *Drum Taps*, the work of Siegfried Sassoon and Wilfred Owen and the already lauded novel and short stories of Ernest Hemingway show war for what it is. One sees it as well in Yevtushenko's "Babii Yar," the powerful work of Anna Akhmatova, Andrey Voznesensky, and in the great Polish master, Czeslaw Milosz. The horrors also show up in the work of dissident writers such as Vasyl Stus and, recently, Carmen Bugan.

In the U. S., the catalogue is extensive and eloquent, from the poems and activist work of Denise Levertov and Allen Ginsberg (among others) to the testimonies of warriors who do not flinch: Bruce Weigl's *Song of Napalm*, Bill Shields' *Post-Vietnam Stress Syndrome*, Andrew Gettler's *Footsteps of a Ghost: Poems from Vietnam*, Robert Borden's 32 part fugue, "Meat Dreams," the Vietnam War poems of Yusef Komunyakaa. The current middle eastern wars have produced at least one master poet, Brian Turner, whose *Here, Bullet* and *Phantom Noise* are historically grounded testimonies of these wars and their effects on all those closely caught up in them.

Poets and writers have been covering what war does to our humanity as long as there have been written words, though there have also been major poems of force, to use Weil's term, which make a virtue of this form of mass murder. Efforts to spur compassion or awareness and to change national priorities and behaviors have alerted many to the need for a different kind of vision, but acknowledged or not, our eloquence has not given legislators the wisdom or tools to effect the desired change. Marxists would of course say this is because such work is part of the superstructure—the articulated ideology—of human life, that the desired effect must be developed in the economic and material bases of human societies, yet even here the "anarchy of production"—true of both capitalist and socialist societies, despite the Marxist claim that only the former suffers from it—and the uncertainties of harvests, the current facts of climate change, the invidious scourge of racism, the deprivations of one class or nation of people and the greed or hunger of others make such end goals problematic. One can only strive to address the problem in whatever ways are available, though at this point in history, I believe hope cannot be a factor in the performance of good works. One must stand fast for what is good in our nature and actions despite the lack of real results, and that is the difficulty in choosing an individual's path in this dark time. Yet it is the only way.

8 April 2019

Works Consulted for this essay

Borden, Robert. "Meat Dreams." *Nada Poems.* David Cope, ed. Grandville, Mi.: Nada, 1988.

Bugan, Carmen. *Burying the Typewriter: Childhood Under the Eye of the Secret Police.* London, Basingstoke and Oxford: Picador/Pan Macmillan, 2012.

- - - - . *The House of Straw.* Bristol: Shearsman, 2014.

- - - - . *Releasing the Porcelain Birds.* Bristol: Shearsman, 2014.

- - - - . *Seamus Heaney and East European Poetry in Translation: Poetics of Exile.* London: Legenda / Modern Humanities Research Association and Maney Publishing, 2013.

Emerson, Ralph Waldo. "Ode Inscribed to William H. Channing." *Poetry Foundation.* [Source: *The Oxford Book of American Poetry.* Oxford University Press, 2006.] Online.

Gandhi, Mohandas K., Mahatma. "Turning the Searchlight Inward." *Gandhi In His Own Words.* Ed. Martin Green. Hanover and London: Tufts U / U Press of New England, 1987.

Ginsberg, Allen. *Collected Poems 1947-1980.* New York, et al: Harper & Row, 1984.

Jefferson, Thomas. "Thomas Jefferson to W. S. Smith, November 13, 1787." *Jefferson and The Rights of Man.* By Dumas Malone. Boston: Little, Brown, 1951. 166.

Komunyakaa, Yusef. *Pleasure Dome: New and Collected Poems.* Middletown, Connecticut: Wesleyan U P, 2001.

Levertov, Denise. *The Collected Poems of Denise Levertov.* New York: New Directions, 2013.

Shakespeare, William. "The Life of Henry the Fifth." *Complete Works.* Jonathan Bate and Eric Rasmussen, eds. New York: Modern Library,

2007.

Shields, Bill. *Post-Vietnam Stress Syndrome.* Brigham, Quebec:
Samisdat, 1988.

Stus, Vasyl. Poems. *Big Scream* 55. Trans. Svitlana Iukhymovych. Ed.
David Cope. Grandville, Mi.: Nada, 2017. 8-21.

Turner, Brian. *Here, Bullet.* Farmington, Maine: Alice James, 2005.

- - - - . *Phantom Noise.* Farmington, Maine: Alice James, 2010.

Weigl, Bruce. *Song of Napalm.* New York: Atlantic Monthly, 1988.

Weil, Simone. The Iliad *or The Poem of Force.* James P. Holoka, ed. and
trans. Critical ed. with essay in both French and English. New York:
Peter Lang, 2008.

Whitman, Walt. "Drum Taps." *Leaves of Grass and Other Writings.*
Michael Moon, ed. New York and London: Norton, 2002. 234-285.

Appendix A: My Essay for Suining
Bridges Across the Pacific: Words Across the Waters

Many in my generation of American poets first learned of Chinese poetry through Ezra Pound's translation of Li Bai's "The Jewel Stairs' Grievance," the translations of Ken Rexroth, Gary Snyder and others, but our real engagement begins with Allen Ginsberg's 1984 visit to China. In my case, Allen sent me a November 11, 1984 postcard that was the forerunner of all that has happened since:

> Dear David: hazy in steamer lounge
> 3'd day down Yangtze River, yesterday
> passed vast mountain gorges and hairpin
> river-bends, mist sun and cement Factory
> soft Coal dust everywhere, all China
> got a big allergic cold. Literary dele-
> gation homebound after 3 weeks, now I'm
> travelling separate like I used to—except
> everywhere omnipresent kindly Chinese
> bureaucracy meets me at airports & boats
> & takes me to tourist hotels & orders meals.
> I'm trying to figure a way out—envious of 2
> bearded hippies travelling 4th class in
> steerage eating Tangerines & bananas—
> sleepers in passageways on mats, Chinese
> voyagers playing checkers. Saw Beijing,
> Great Wall, tombs & palaces, Suchow's
> Tang Gardens, Hangchow's West Lake walkway
> dyke to hold the giant water in the years of drought
> built by governors of Tsu-Tung-Po and Po-Chu-I.
> Saw Cold Mt. Temple w/ Snyder who'd
> heard its bell echo across years.
>
> Love Allen Ginsberg

I published this as a poem in the twentieth issue of my *Big Scream* (1985), but Allen's visit awakened Chinese scholars and poets to the possibility of *sharing* the path that poetry can open up to greater understanding and kindness.

The historical connections between us all develop in the translations of Kerouac and Ginsberg by Professor Wen Chu-an of Sichuan University. The dialogue grows toward our generation in Wen Chu-an's work with Vernon Frazer and later, with Jim Cohn's efforts to develop an anthology which Wen could translate. Frazer attended the 2004 "Beat Meets East: an International Interdisciplinary Conference on the Age of Spontaneity" (Dialogue 66), made possible by the "vision and commitment" of Wen Chu-an and Bill Lawlor (Ball). Gordon Ball's keynote address set the tone, exploring the influence of the East on American literary masters, especially in the poems of Bai Juyi (Po Chu-I) on Allen Ginsberg.

After the conference, Frazer went on to read his poems in both Beijing and Nanjing (Zhang, Dialogue 66). Zhang Ziqing's "Dialogue" establishes his connection with Frazer: after Vernon's reading, he drove Frazer and his wife around Nanjing. Later, Vernon published *The Selected Poems of the Postbeats* in Beijing (2008), an anthology warmly received in China as "a kind of new poetry which is a continuation and development of Beat poetry after the death of Allen Ginsberg" (quoted in Zhang , Dialogue 67).

Also in 2004, Jim Cohn wrote Wen Ch-an to ask if they could work together on an anthology introducing Chinese readers to translations of Postbeat American poets "after receiving a copy of his 2001 Chinese/ English bilingual edition of *Howl: Allen Ginsberg: Selected Poems (1947-1997)*" (Cohn, "All Loves"). Jim's September request led to active dialogue, and by December

Wen received a contents, description of the proposed project, a revised introduction, and bios. After a good beginning, there was a long hiatus when Jim no longer received answers to his queries, and in 2009, Vernon Frazer shared the news that Wen had died of a heart attack.

Jim's and my connection to Professor Zhang Ziqing begins in the work done with Wen Chu-an. Zhang was "an editor on contemporary American literature in English Language for *Contemporary Foreign Literature*," and he published Wen's introduction of Postbeat poetry "with his translation of some Postbeat poems for the first time in China." He notes, "unfortunately, his sudden death interrupted the anthology. As a friend of his, I had to continue his project with writing a preface and adding a few more Postbeat poets. Then Vernon introduced you [David] and Jim to me when I began to add a chapter on Postbeat poetry to my book *A History of 20th Century American Poetry*" (Zhang, email to David Cope). Frazer had asked Zhang to read Jim's essay, "Postbeat Poets" (Cohn, Postbeat). Jim later collaborated with him, "adding a number of 20th and 21st century Chinese poets to MAP's international exhibits" (All Loves). The anthology eventually fell by the wayside, but Zhang included a chapter on the Postbeat poets in his study of contemporary American poetry, with translations and discussion of some of our poems. He eventually suggested the idea for a bilingual empathy anthology of Chinese and American poets, and Jim and I began collecting American poems. After 2013, we made little progress on the work until Zhang began choosing from my poems for a selection that he intended to translate and publish. Thus began a three month period of questions and answers concerning my lines, words, and phrases, all with the idea of "getting it right" in Chinese.

The project, entitled *Bridges Across the Pacific,* was complicated by different cultural understandings of the term "empathy," and the concern that some American publishers wanted large fees for republishing their poets' work. We were working for free and had no funds, and Zhang was having his own problems trying to find a Chinese publisher who would take on the project. We put the idea on hold, continuing in a different way. Zhang translated and published several of the American poets in the *Journal of Jianghan University*, and in my case, published my poems in *Poetry Periodical* and in *Houston Garden of Verses.* When my book *The Invisible Keys* was published, he introduced me to scholars Sun Hong and Wang Guanglin, who both wrote perceptive reviews of my work which appeared in two respected American journals. Zhang also introduced me to his former student, Dong (Peter) Feng, whose poems appeared in my journal, *Big Scream.*

I come at last to Suining through the graces of *Poetry Periodical,* and with thanks to Zhang. I am here to *learn* through our dialogues and silences, giving thanks for this time together, opening ways to "make it new," finding kindnesses and compassion that are central to the best poetry in this world.

David 戴维研讨会文章中文附件

Ginsberg's post card for David:

金斯堡甚至 1984 年在中国教学和旅行时，都不忘给科普寄明信片，报告他的近况，其中一张明信片，科普把它排列在诗歌形式：

1984 年 11 月 11 日星期天下午

亲爱的戴维：在朦胧的轮船休息室里

长江上朝下游驶去第三天，

昨天通过三峡，发夹似的

弯曲河道，朦胧的阳光，水泥厂

处处煤尘四起，全中国得了

过敏性大感冒。文学代表团

在三个星期之后回国了，像

惯常一样，分开后，我此刻

独自旅行——除了无所不在的

友好的中国官方人士在机场

和轮船会见我，陪我到旅游

酒店，帮我订餐。我想弄明白

眼前的情况——羡慕两个坐

四等舱的留胡须的嬉皮士

在统舱里吃着香蕉和橘子——

一些旅客坐在通道的垫子上

下跳棋。游览了北京，长城；

苏州园林；杭州西湖的长堤，

苏东坡和白居易做官时在干旱

年代为蓄水而筑的堤坝。看到了

苏州寒山寺，斯奈德听到了

千年钟声的回响。

爱你　艾伦·金斯堡

——张子清译

Wen Chu-an 文楚安

Sun Hong　孙宏

Wang Guanglin 王光林

Dong Feng 冯冬

Zhang 张子清

戴维·科普（David Cope）

吉姆·科恩（**Jim Cohn**）

弗农·弗雷泽（**Vernon Frazer**）

后垮掉派诗选》，上海 人民出版社，**2008**

(*Selected Poems of Postbeat Poets* edited by Vernon Frazer)

江汉学术》（**Journal of Jianghan University**）

北京《诗刊》（*Poetry Periodical*）

休斯敦诗苑》(Houston Garden of Verses)

Works Consulted in Bridges Across the Pacific essay

Ball, Gordon. Keynote Address, *Beat Meets East: International Conference on Literature in the Age of Spontaneity*. Chengdu, Sichuan, China: Sichuan University. 3 June 2004.

Cohn, Jim. "All Loves Are The Way Onward: Interview With Kirpal Gordon." *The Museum Of American Poetics*. Online. 18 February, 2012.

- - - - . Email to Wen Chu-an. 8 September 2004.

- - - - . "Postbeat Poets." Postbeat Poets Activist Scholarship Project." *The Museum of American Poetics*. Online. Originally published at *Wikipedia: The Free Encyclopedia*. January 8, 2008. This revised version published in *Sutras & Bardos: Essays and Interviews on Allen Ginsberg, The Kerouac School, Anne Waldman, Postbeat Poets and The New Demotics*. Boulder: Museum of American Poetics Publications, 2011.

Cope, David. "Bridges Across the Pacific: A Chinese [and] American Empathy Anthology." Interview by Kirpal Gordon. *Taking Giant Steps* Online Blog.

Frazer, Vernon. "Extending the Age of Spontaneity to a New Era: Post-Beat Poets in America." Beat Meets East: Presentations from a Conference. *Big Bridge* 10. Ed. Michael Rothenberg. Online.

- - - - . "Post-Beat Poetry in China." Preface. *Selected Poems of Post-Beat Poets*. Beijing: Shanghai Century Publications, 2008. *Big Bridge 14* (2009). Online.

Ginsberg, Allen. *Clear Seeing Poetics*. Unpublished classroom anthology, selected by Allen Ginsberg; includes some of the poems he taught in China. Undated.

- - - - . "[Poem] 3'd day down Yangtze River, yesterday." *Wait Till I'm Dead: Uncollected Poems*. Ed. Bill Morgan. New York: Grove Press, 2016. Previously published in *Big Scream* 20. Ed. David Cope. Grandville, Mi.:

Nada Press, 1985.

"Ginsberg and China." *The Allen Ginsberg Project.* Online blog. 9 September 2017.

Huang Jie Han. "On the Rewritings of *On the Road* in China." Guizhou
    University. Masters Thesis. Abstract. 2008. Online. Dissertation
    Topic 736213.

Jones, Jim. "How the Beats Came to China." *Gadfly Online.* Charlottesville, Va.:
    Gadfly Productions, 1998-2009. Online.

Meyer, Mike. "The World's Biggest Book Market." With quotes from Wen Chu'an
    on Ginsberg and Kerouac. *The New York Times* (13 March 2005). N.p.

Min yu. "Allen Ginsberg and China." *Theory and Practice in Language Studies* 2.4
    (April, 2012): 850-855. Online. Academy Publication.

Pound, Ezra. "The Jewel Stairs' Grievance." *Personae.* New Directions, 1926, 1935,
    1971. 132.

"Wen Chu-an." Biography. *The Museum of American Poetics.* Postbeat Poets section.
    Online.

Wen Chu-an. "Letter from China." *The Blacklisted Journalist.* Letter copyright Al
    Aronowitz, to whom it was addressed. Online. Column 58e. 2001.

Wen Chu-an, trans. *Howl: Allen Ginsberg: Selected Poems (1947-1997).*
    Sichuan: Sichuan Literature and Art Publishing House, 2000.

- - - -, trans. *On the Road.* Guilin Shi: Li Jiang chuban she, 2001. World Cat Online.

"Zhang Ziqing." Biography. *The Museum of American Poetics.* Postbeat Poets
    section. Online.

Zhang Ziqing. "A Dialogue between Chinese and American Poets in the New
    Century: Their Poetry Reading, Translation and Writing in Collaboration."
    Comparative Literature: East West 15.2 (Autumn/Winter 2011): 65-81.
    Sichuan University, Chengdu, China.

- - - - . Email to David Cope. 17 September 2015.

- - - - . Email to Jim Cohn. 5 March 2010.

- - - - . "On American Postbeat Poetry." *Journal of Jianghan University.*

Wuhan, China. 408-418. In Chinese. Print.

- - - - , trans. "In Silence." By David Cope. *Houston Garden of Verses* 5
      (2018.02) 7.

- - - - , trans. Nine poems. By David Cope. *Poetry Periodical* 1. Zhao Si, ed.
      Beijing: Peoples' Republic of China, 2018.

Appendix B: My Presentation at the March 5 Dialogue

First, in response to national poetic style, I feel that one should speak of a nation's <u>poetries</u>, not poetry—many styles, many kinds of minds and approaches to practice, many trajectories through a life borne of real experiences.

I believe in the absolute equality of women, ethnic, disability poets, and immigrants, among others, both in terms of ways of making poems and in equal representation in publications. China has many minorities, and it would be a great enrichment to have their cultural particulars represented as part of the great quilt that makes up the nation's cultures. Under-represented cultures bring their words and phrases into the mainstream, as well as kinds of writing particular to their cultural experiences and history, lending their particular kinds of wisdom and precision to the larger whole.

There is risk and reward for those with power when we accept this kind of equality. Their experience may involve class and ethnic suffering, and they do need to share their perspectives if a nation is to fully understand itself, and to address its real needs. This openness to their experiences is absolutely necessary if one is to live by the idea of absolute equality for all—even if it makes those with power uncomfortable.

Last, I want to thank Chinese scholars who have contributed to the development of post-beat poets in my generation. Our cross-cultural dialogues have enriched us all and given us a finer appreciation for each other, for our languages and our nations' gifts. These are Wen Chu-an of Sichuan University, the one who picked up on Allen Ginsberg's efforts to develop a dialogue in China; Zhang Ziqing of Nanjing University, who followed up on the editing and translating efforts begun by Wen, later translating my work and publishing it here, perhaps the single most important development that made my journey here possible; and two professors whose reviews of my new and selected poems, *The Invisible Keys*, are among the most perceptive writings about my work in my entire career: Sun Hong of Renming University, and Wang Guanglin, from Shanghai International Studies University, and Vice President, the Chinese Association for Australian Studies. THANK-YOU.

Appendix C:

Poems for Suining International Poetry Week

Translations and Footnotes by Professor Zhang Ziqing

2-6 March 2019

Contents:

在 沉 默 中--致安·巴伯 （外三首）

（美国）戴维·科普
张子清 译

一小时又一小时
他们在急诊室等待着，
期待伤残者

滚滚洪流的到来——
但是，只有消防队员

他们吸入烟雾，
带着伤口和擦伤，一小时
又一小时，时光

在流逝，灰尘
飞扬，填塞着
冬天花园，

棕榈中庭，那里没有
伤员行走，也没有
救护员背着伤残者

只有静默，终于
明白不会有人
从开着的门

进来，而门外的远处
传来尖叫，悲鸣，
无尽的喧嚣。

In Silence
for Ann Barber

hour after hour
they waited in the ER,
expecting the onrush

of wounded & maimed—
yet there were only
  firefighters with

smoke inhalation,
cuts & bruises, hour after
hour, the minutes

ticking away, the dust not
even settled, filling
the winter garden, the palm

court, where no
wounded walked nor
rescuers bore the maimed,

only the silence &
the realization at last
that none would come

thru the open door,
beyond the shrieks & sighs
& the endless roar.

By David Cope (2001. From *Turn the Wheel.* Humana, 2003.)

阿迪朗达克[1]月亮

营火熄灭了——帐篷门帘开着
两个朋友[2]陷入沉思，然后谈着话：

满月的月光穿过
铁杉树纤细的手指——

稍远处浓密的橙色桦树叶在
微风中啪嗒啪嗒地紧贴一起——

甚至苔藓、蕨类植物和
无皮的树干在月光中闪耀，

古代莫霍克人梦中有同样的
星星，有同样闪光的树叶

---

[1] 指美国最大的荒野地，面积比几个州还大，甚至也比有些国家大，几乎与比利时的面积相等。但是它又紧靠美国人口最密集的地方——离纽约市仅 320 公里。现为阿迪朗达克州立公园（Adirondack）。

[2] 指作者和他的朋友吉姆·科恩。吉姆对此回忆说："这是一次非常棒的秋天露营，树叶全是金色和红色，我和戴维这时在一起好像是李白与杜甫。"——见吉姆 2015 年 6 月月 16 日发送给译者的 e-mail 回复。

纷纷飘到洒满月光的

泥地上——谁知道

当睁眼睡觉的人翻身时

何处是醒的结束梦的开始？

Adirondack Moon

the fire's out—tentflap open,
two friends muse & talk:

full moon thru delicate
fingers of hemlock—

orange birch leafclouds beyond,
clinging in a whipping breeze—

even mosses & ferns & barkless
trunks shine in this light,

same stars in ancient Mohawk
dream, same flash of leaves

sailing to earth across
moonstruck land—who knows

where waking ends & dreams begin
as open-eyed sleepers turn?

By David Cope (October, 1990. From *Coming Home*. Humana, 1993.)

劳作

渔夫的自行车
躺倒在地。他快速
投出他的钓线。

鸬鹚低飞，
在黑黝黝的水上搜索。
天鹅仍然
伏在她的巢中。

有多少次
我从这里转弯，
对着耀眼的

水波，
朝远处的山岗
跑去？

很快就会回到家
查看花园，在那里
我的粗制靴子

将来回走动，跪在地上
种植金黄色的鱼尾菊，
紫色红色的天竺葵。

相同的初夏之风

吹拂我的皮肤和脸颊。

前面依然有劳作等我。

The Work

the fisherman's bike lies
where it fell. He is
quick to cast his line.

cormorants fly low,
searching the dark water.
the swan is still

on her nest. how many
times have I rounded
this corner, racing

to the hill beyond,
blind to bright
shine on the waves?

soon I'll be home,
survey the garden where
my rough boots will

tramp, where I'll kneel
& plant golden zinnias,
heliotrope, red geraniums,

same early summer winds
caressing my skin & cheeks,
the work *still* before me.

By David Cope (2015. From *The Invisible Keys: New and Selected Poems.* Ghost Pony, 2018.)

三月的祝福[3]

阳光闪耀的洪水，平静如镜：

成千上万的小树苗弯向洪水线

一直伸向天空

树木上挂着漂浮物、树叶、枝条、

泡沫塑料杯、风从高速公路上

刮来的报纸和包装袋。

一座座古老的墓冢成了孤岛：⁴

这片土地上古老的灵魂们

在他们的尸骨和骷颅之上歌唱——

花儿含苞欲放，一只只乌鸦

从高高的树枝上朝下盯视，

风温暖而新鲜，足以让

一个忙碌的旅人调头看，

在他的梦里响起轻松的歌，

听洪水退落：我梦见了

　　　早已离世的你！回想起

　　　你赤裸裸狂奔，指望

³ 指对作者的早已去世的朋友托德和在托德去世后三月份出生的儿子的祝福。作者如今把儿子威尔带来一同拜
　谒托德，托德地下有知，一定会很高兴。——见诗人 2015 年 5 月 18 日发送给译者的 e-mail 回复。

⁴ 指霍普韦尔印第安人在 1100-1200 年筑在河边的沼泽中的墓冢，被印第安人认为是圣地。在春天，河水经常
　泛滥的洪水，达 5-10 英尺深，当这种情况发生时，墓冢便成了岛屿。——见诗人 2015 年 5 月 18 日发送给译
　者的 e-mail 回复。

你依然和我在一起，
静静地站在这里，

我带着儿子第一次来到这河岸
来看野鸟的飞翔，来认沙土上
留下的足迹和痕迹，来听

那空旷无声的旋律，来呼吸
那条河祝福的气息。

A March Blessing

sunsparkled floodwaters, glassy calm:
thousands of saplings bent at floodline
straighten to run at the sky! Fallen

trees are draped with flotsam, leaves
& sticks & Styrofoam cups, papers
& wrappers blown from the highway.

the old mounds are islands now:
ancient spirits sing in this land
above their bones & flooded skulls—

first buds swell, great ravens
stare from high branches, the wind
is just warm & fresh enough to turn

a busy traveler's head & fill
his dream with lazy song, hear that
falling water now; so I dream of you,

long gone! recall you racing naked
paths & count you still as one with me
here silently as I bring my son

to this shore for the first time,
to see the wild flights of birds &
know the tracks & signs in sand,

hear that open, quiet melody, breathe
that breath of river's blessing,
that calm & rising, falling flow.

By David Cope (1990. From *Coming Home*. Humana, 1993.)

Appendix D: Video Script for Poetic Suining

I am David Cope, and I bring
Greetings to Poetic Suining.

Let Suining gather a great
harvest from poets' minds,
& give voice to a peoples' song.

May we make this journey
with dignity and grace,
may we honor our poems
& the poems of friends,
sing with new spirits whose
lines shake us all awake.

Let us honor the spirit
of our peoples, sit quietly,
sit humbly in the halls

& gardens of ancient China,
honor her people, her
ancestors, her history,

the many tales that make up
a nation's heart & song.
Let us enter a new world
with open eyes & ears,
our hearts free to share
& receive kindness,

unforeseeable passage
come at last, spirit of sages—
Walt Whitman be with us all.

Annotated Sources Consulted for My Visit to China

Alley, Rewi, trans. *Bai Juyi: 200 Selected Poems.* Beijing: New World Press, 1983. [a.k.a Po Chǔ-I. This is likely the edition read by Allen Ginsberg for his 1984 visit to China, which resulted, among other poems, in "Reading Bai Juyi." David S. Wills writes in "The Mystery of Allen Ginsberg's 'Reading Bai Juyi'" that "On December 5th, 1984, while laid up sick in Shanghai, Allen Ginsberg wrote one of his lesser-known masterpieces, "Reading Bai Juyi." The poem begins by talking about Allen's first month in China, where he had been teaching and travelling after a short visit with a delegation of American writers, and ends with a short biographical piece that copies a poem by Tang Dynasty poet, Bai Juyi." Online.

Bardo, Cheryl, The Field Museum. *China: A History.* New York: Abrams Books for Young Readers, 2018. [A colorful book with sketchy overview of Chinese history, mainly useful as a contextual guide to the exhibits in Chicago's Field Museum display of Chinese history and culture.]

Cai, Zong-Qi. *How to Read Chinese Poetry in Context: Poetic Culture from Antiquity Through the T'ang.* New York: Columbia U P, 2018.

Chaves, Jonathan, trans. and ed. *The Columbia Book of Later Chinese Poetry (Yǔan, Ming, and Ch'ing Dynasties (1279-1911).* New York: Columbia, 1986. [See Burton Watson, below, for the first volume in this series].

"Chen Zi'ang." *Wikipedia.* Online. 16 July 2019. [overview and brief bio of the poet, noting his importance as T'ang period predecessor. See Ho, Richard M. W. reference in this list for comprehensive study of the poet's work].

Cope, David. "David Cope on Editing *Bridges Across the Pacific: A Chinese*

/ *American Empathy Anthology*." Interviewed by Kirpal Gordon. *Taking Giant Steps*. Blog. 20 September 2015. Online.

- - - - . Review of Wang Ping's *Ten Thousand Waves*. *Paterson Literary Review*. Vol. 43. 2015-2016. Pages 265-268.

Deneke, Wiebke, Li Wai-Yee, and Tian Xiaofei. *The Oxford Handbook of Classical Chinese Literature (1000 BCE-900 CE)*. New York: Oxford U P, 2017. [As with all Oxford handbooks and guides, best taken a chapter at a time, as needed].

Graham, A. C., trans. *Poems of the Late T'ang*. New York: Penguin, 1965; New York: New York Review of Books, 1977.

"Guan Yin." *Wikipedia*. Online. 16 July 2019. [overview of the deity's importance in the Buddhist pantheon, with key texts and bibliography. No mention here of her importance to Suining as citizen/daughter and city icon, nor of the two great temples that are central to the area's social fabric]

Ha Jin. *The Banished Immortal: A Life of Li Bai*. New York: Pantheon, 2019. [Superbly researched yet extremely readable biography of the great poet].

Hamill, Sam. *Crossing the River: Three Hundred Poems from the Chinese*. Rochester, New York: Tiger Bark, 2013. [An eminently readable book of translations by an important American poet and editor].

Hawkes, David, trans. *Songs of the South: An Ancient Chinese Anthology of Poems By Qu Yuan and Other Poets*. London, New York, et al: Penguin, 2011. [Key early text, important as background for Wang Ping's famed paean and lament for China, *Ten Thousand Waves*: see Wang Ping, below, and David Cope for review],

Hinton, David, trans. *The Late Poems of Wang An-Shih*. New York: New Directions, 2015.

- - - - , trans. *The Mountain Poems of Meng Hao-jan*. New York: Archipelago

Books, 2004.

- - - - , trans. *The Selected Poems of Li Po.* New York: New Directions, 1996.
    [A.k.a Li Bai].

- - - - , trans. *The Selected Poems of Tu Fu.* New York: New Directions, 1989.
    [The book I pored over again and again, getting to know Du Fu as poet
    and man. Hinton is an excellent translator, worthy to stand beside Bill
    Porter].

- - - - , trans. *The Selected Poems of Wang Wei.* New York: New Directions,
    2006.

- - - - , trans. *The Selected Poems of Po Chű-I.* New York: New Directions, 1999.
    [a.k.a Bai Juyi].

Ho, Richard M. W. *Ch'en Tzu-Ang: Innovator in T'ang Poetry.* Hong Kong:
    The Chinese University Press, 1993. [Presently, this volume contains the
    most definitive study of Chen's work, and the most complete set of
    translations of his poems into English. I surmise a much more
    comprehensive study of the poet in the future, however, as Mr. Su, chair
    of the Chen Zi'ang Academy and Research Center, notes that current
    researchers have newly gathered a total of 81 volumes of Chen's works for
    study and research.]

Hung, William. *Tu Fu: China's Greatest Poet.* Cambridge: Harvard U P, 1952.
    [Still the biography of note in English, David Hinton draws extensively
    from Hung's account in the Biography section of *The Selected Poems of Tu
    Fu*].

Idema, Wilt, and Beata Grant, eds. *The Red Brush: Writing Women of Imperial
    China.* Cambridge and London: Harvard U Asia Center, 2004. [Definitive
    collection of women's poetry, over 900 pages of work written over the
    millennia of Chinese literary history].

Lau, D. C., trans. *Mencius.* London, New York, et al., 1970.

Lenfestey, James P. *Seeking the Cave: A Pilgrimage to Cold Mountain.*

Minneapolis: Milkweed Editions, 2014. [James P. Lenfestey's *Seeking the Cave: A Pilgrimage to Cold Mountain is* a classic text in the genre of poets' travel journals, setting the bar for the best of such works. Lenfestey's journey is both illuminative of the wisdom gained through attentive and disciplined travel via the struggles he and his companions went through to find and do proper homage to great poets of China, with the ultimate triumph of their efforts coming when they visited the cave and haunts of Han Shan, Cold Mountain. Lenfestey had been fascinated with the wisdom of Cold Mountain ever since he first encountered the mysterious wild man's elusive poetry, and this journey ultimately becomes one of standing where the great predecessor stood, and of fully exploring his own spiritual center. Written in the form of a haibun modified to include poetry typical of Chinese traditions, the book is also in the tradition of western prosimetric masterpieces such as Boethius's *Consolation of Philosophy* and Dante's *Vita Nuova* and *Convivio*—all such works featuring a mixture of poetry and prose, in which each form extends or comments on the other. Lenfestey's book features both his own original poems responding to his experiences, and translated poetry by those poets whose graves and haunts he visits. The book also gives us a delightful grasp of his fellow travelers, with this reader's special delight in his observation of his most famed companion, the great translator and pilgrim to China, Bill Porter. Indeed, it could be said that Lenfestey's volume could make a fine companion to Porter's own classic work, *Finding Them Gone: Visiting China's Poets of the Past*.

Lennon, John. "Meat City." *Mind Games*. CD. Capitol Records, CD reissue of 1973 album..

Lin, Shuen-Fu, and Stephen Owen, eds. *The Vitality of the Lyric Voice: Shih Poetry from The Late Han to the T'ang*. Princeton: Princeton

U P, 1986.

Porter, Bill / Red Pine. *Finding Them Gone: Visiting China's Poets of the Past.*
Port Townsend, Wa.: Copper Canyon, 2016. [Bill Porter is one of the
finest of contemporary translators of the classic bards of the T'ang era,
but this volume takes the reader a step farther: in a very readable
travelogue, he takes us on a journey to the poets' graves and/or
memorials, translates important poems by each author and places the
translated poems in the context of their lives and the cultural milieu in
which they lived. He honors them in his own inimitable way, showers
them with the praise deserved by the great poets of literature, and
journeys to the next poet's final resting place, giving us access to a
different mind, a different kind of life, and the words to understand
what a great heart and command of words can do to bring the struggles
and meanings that a life may have—to bring us finally to ponder our own
time on this earth. This is a very deep and sincere set of homages, unlike
anything I've ever seen in the field of poetry.]

- - - - , trans. *The Collected Songs of Cold Mountain.* Revised and expanded
edition. Port Townsend, Wa.: Copper Canyon, 2000.
[Perhaps this is the standard edition of our time, though I readily
admit that I tend to gravitate to the Gary Snyder translations which
first made me aware of Han Shan's great collection of poems.]

- - - - , trans. *Poems of the Masters: China's Classic Anthology of T'ang
and Sung Dynasty Verse.* Port Townsend, Wa.: Copper Canyon, 2003.

Rexroth, Kenneth, and Ling Ching, trans. *Li Ch'ing-chao: Complete Poems.*
New York: New Directions, 1979. [A.k.a Li Qingzhao. China's greatest
woman poet].

- - - - , trans. *Women Poets of China.* New York: New Directions, 1972.
[The translators are to be commended for bringing a collection of
women poets to publication in the U. S. this early in the translation

of China's great poets].

Slingerland, Edward. *Confucius Analects: With Selections from Traditional Commentaries.* Indianapolis and Cambridge: Hackett, 2003.

Snyder, Gary. *Riprap and Cold Mountain Poems.* 50th Anniversary ed. Berkeley: Counterpoint, 2009.

Some Poetries. Pamphlet of conference essays by participants. Suining, China: Suining International Poetry Week, March 2019. [Requested essays by conference participants, most in their own languages].

Waley, Arthur, trans. *Translations from the Chinese.* New York: Knopf, 1941. [For decades, the standard translations used by American poets and readers—still an important source and a memorable touchstone in translation literature].

- - - -, and Joseph R. Allen, trans. *The Book of Songs: The Ancient Chinese Classic of Poetry.* New York: Grove, 1966. [Key early text, important, too, for understanding Chen Zi'ang's Confucian ethics of poetry and his insistence on clarity and accessibility].

Wang Ping. *Ten Thousand Waves.* San Antonio: Wings, 2014.

- - - -, ed. *New Generation: Poems from China Today.* Brooklyn: Hanging Loose, 1999.

Watson, Burton, trans. and ed. *The Columbia Book of Chinese Poetry: From Early Times to the Thirteenth Century.* New York: Columbia, 1984. [For decades, this was my "go-to" book when first exploring the work of a given poet, before my research went more deeply into individual masters, biographies, and critical writings. Still an important touchstone. See Jonathan Chaves, for the second volume in this collection].

Wilkinson, Endymion. *Chinese History: A New Manual.* Fifth ed. Cambridge: Harvard U Asia Center, 2018. [A tome-like veritable encyclopedia of Chinese history and culture, this volume is

superbly organized and the reader can access authoritative brief
but very careful descriptions of subject matter and, more importantly,
key sources worth pursuing. I found this book particularly
useful when researching Chinese feminism and literature, discovering
The Red Brush (Idema and Grant, above) through the list of sources
here].

Wu, John C. H. *Four Seasons of T'ang Poetry*. Rutland, Vermont, and
Tokyo: Charles E. Tuttle, 1972.

Zhang Ziqing. *A History of 20th Century American Poetry*. Three Vols.
Published in China, 2019. [For items involving the "Postbeat Poets"—
my generation of American outrider poets—see Chapter 22 in Volume 2
(pages 1306-1380, with an extensive set of photos at the beginning of
Volume 1. This history is Zhang's masterwork and the labor of decades].

- - - - . "On American Postbeat Poetry." *Journal of Jianghan University*.
2015. Pages 408-418. With the work of David Cope, Jim Cohn and other
poets, and bibliography.

- - - - , trans. "In Silence," by David Cope. *Houston Garden of Verses*. Vol. 5. 2018.
Page 7.

- - - - , trans. Nine poems by David Cope. *Poetry Periodical* (Beijing). 2018.
Pages 58-61.

David Cope

Born 1948, Detroit, Mi. Education: BA University of Michigan, MA+30 Western Michigan University. Married 49 years, 3 grown children. Taught Shakespeare, Drama, Creative Writing, Multicultural Literature, Women's Studies, etc. at Grand Rapids Community College for 22 years; school custodian 18 years before that. Kent County Dyer Ives Poetry Competition, first place adult category winner, 1971, 1972. Pushcart Prize winner, 1977. Distinguished Alumni award, GRCC 1984. Seven books and two chapbooks published, winner of award in literature from American Academy/Institute of Arts and Letters, 1988. Editor and publisher, *Big Scream* magazine, 1974-2019+. Poet Laureate of Grand Rapids, Mi. 2011-2014; editor of three anthologies: *Nada Poems* (Nada, 1988), *Sunflowers & Locomotives: Songs for Allen* (elegies for Allen Ginsberg, Nada, 1998), and *Song of the Owashtanong: Grand Rapids Poetry in the 21st Century* (Ridgeway, 2013). In 2017, David completed *The Correspondence of David Cope and Allen Ginsberg (1976-1996)*, still unpublished. 2017-2018 publications include *The Train:* "Howl" *in Chicago* (chapbook, Multifarious Press, 2017), and *The Invisible Keys: New and Selected Poems* 1975-2017 (Ghost Pony Press, 2018). Also in 2018, David's "In Silence" appeared in Chinese translation by Professor Zhang Ziqing as part as group of 9-11 poems in *Houston Garden of Verses*, and nine of his poems were included in translations by Zhang in *Poetry Periodical* (Beijing). Dr. Peter Feng also translated two of Cope's poems for a Chinese online poetry journal, *Poetry Sky*. In 2019, David's poems were translated and discussed in vol. II (1379-1386) of Professor Zhang's three volume study, *A History of 20th Century American Poetry*. Cope was the only American poet conferee at the Suining International Poetry Week and Chen Zi'ang Poetry Awards in Sichuan, China (March, 2019). His work from that journey appears in *A Bridge Across the Pacific* (A Jabber Publication, 2020), and the essays and international dialogue from the book are published by *Rabbit: A Journal of Non-fiction Poetry* (Australia). His "River Rouge" appears in *RESPECT: The Poetry of Detroit Music*, ed. Jim Daniels and M. L. Liebler (Michigan State University Press, 2020). The David Cope Papers (1972-2013) are maintained at the University of Michigan Special Collections Library, and his webpage, The Dave Cope Sampler, is online at the Museum of American Poetics.

Other Works from
A Jabber Publication

"Jon Dambacher" (green) by Jon Dambacher
"Jon Dambacher" (brown) by Jon Dambacher
"Buster" by Jon Dambacher
"Daffy" by Cliff Weber
"first fig" by Erin Dillon
"Scream as You Leave" by Ian Winterbuaer
"Hearingaid!" by Jon Dambacher
"Lost City Highway" by Jake St. John
"The Further Adventures of Scheib" by Cliff Weber